The Back of Beyond

Meriwether Lewis

William Clark

The Back of Beyond

A Story about Lewis and Clark

by Andy Russell Bowen
illustrations by Ralph L. Ramstad

A Carolrhoda Creative Minds Book

Carolrhoda Books, Inc./Minneapolis

For Bob, whose knowledge and love of the West helped me to follow the trail of Lewis and Clark—A.B.

To my wife, Ruth, and those of my family who tolerated and even encouraged my Lewis and Clark obsession for months!—R.R.

Text copyright © 1997 by Andy Russell Bowen
Illustration copyright © 1997 by Ralph L. Ramstad
Map on pp. 6–7 by John Erste, copyright © Lerner Publications Company.
All rights reserved. International copyright secured. No part of this book
may be reproduced, stored in a retrieval system, or transmitted in any
form or by any means, electronic, mechanical, photocopying, recording,
or otherwise, without the prior written permission of Carolrhoda Books,
Inc., except for the inclusion of brief quotations in an acknowledged
review.

This book is available in two editions:
Library binding by Carolrhoda Books, Inc.
Soft cover by First Avenue Editions, 1997
c/o The Lerner Publishing Group
241 First Avenue North
Minneapolis, MN 55401 U.S.A.

Library of Congress Cataloging-in-Publication Data

Bowen, Andy Russell.
    The back of beyond: a story about Lewis and Clark / by Andy
Russell Bowen ; illustrations by Ralph L. Ramstad.
        p.   cm. — (A Carolrhoda creative minds book)
    Includes bibliographical references and index.
    Summary: An account of the 1804–1806 Lewis and Clark Expedition
which took the explorers from St. Louis to the Pacific Ocean.
    ISBN 0-57505-010-2 (lib. bdg.)
    ISBN 1-57505-224-5 (pbk.)
    1. Lewis and Clark Expedition (1804–1806)—Juvenile literature.
2. Lewis, Meriwether, 1774–1809—Juvenile literature. 3. Clark, William,
1770–1838—Juvenile literature. [1. Lewis and Clark Expedition
(1804–1806) 2. Lewis, Meriwether, 1774–1809. 3. Clark, William,
1770–1838. 4. Explorers.] I. Ramstad, Ralph L., 1919–   ill. II. Title.
III. Series.
F592.7.B67   1997
917.804'2—dc20
                                                        95-51267

Manufactured in the United States of America
1 2 3 4 5 6 – JR – 02 01 00 99 98 97

Table of Contents

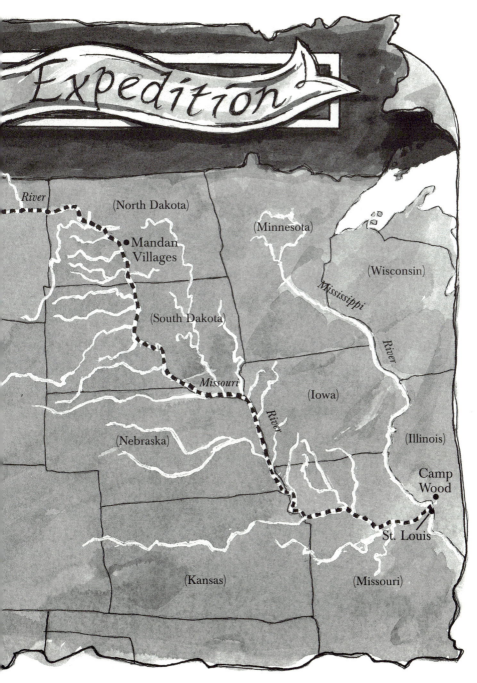

Current state names are in parentheses.

① A Voyage of Discovery

In the rolling foothills of the Blue Ridge Mountains near Charlottesville, Virginia, was a plantation called Locust Hill. It belonged to a family named Lewis. On August 18, 1774, less than a year before the start of the American Revolution, their second child was born, a son called Meriwether.

Meriwether was a bright youngster, always eager to learn. His father, William, taught him the family motto: "To the brave man, everything he does is for his country." His mother, Lucy, taught him the important lessons of honesty, loyalty, fairness, and obedience.

William Lewis died in 1779, leaving his wife to raise their three young children. Lucy soon remarried and a few years later moved her family to Georgia. The plantation was left in the care of relatives. Meriwether's mother tutored him at home until he was thirteen and then sent him back to Virginia, where he received private instruction in math, astronomy, and geography. He lived at Locust Hill, which he had inherited after his father's death. At the age of eighteen, Meriwether gave up his studies to manage the plantation full-time.

The plantation's closest neighbor, just across a field of chattering locusts, was a grand estate called Monticello. It belonged to a country gentleman named Thomas Jefferson, who had known the Lewis family for a long time. Mr. Jefferson was a well-educated man, full of energy and curiosity. Over the next few years, he became better acquainted with Meriwether and was impressed with the young man's determination and intelligence.

When Meriwether was twenty years old, he left home for a taste of military life. It was the summer of 1794, and President George Washington was having trouble with a group of Pennsylvania farmers who were distilling some of their corn crops into whiskey. The farmers refused to pay the tax that Congress had placed on their home brew, and they awaited the revenue collectors with rifles at the ready. Meriwether joined the special troops called in by the president to enforce the tax. The Whiskey Rebellion, as the incident came to be called, was soon put down, but it lasted long enough to give Meriwether a liking for the army. Before long he became a full-time soldier.

The following year, Meriwether was transferred to a unit called the Chosen Rifle Company, where he trained as a sharpshooter under the command of an officer named William Clark. Although the Lewis and Clark families had both lived near Charlottesville at one time, Meriwether and William had never met. During the six months they served together, the two men became friends. But their lives took them in separate directions, and they didn't meet again until 1803.

In 1801, Meriwether left the army to accept a job as private secretary to Thomas Jefferson, newly elected president of the United States. The salary was five hundred dollars a year, and Lewis was allowed to retain his rank of army captain. The two men worked well together, and Meriwether spent many long evenings listening to Jefferson talk about his hopes for the country's future.

The president spoke of the vast region that stretched from the Mississippi River to the western coast. White settlers called the land the Great Unknown, the End of the Earth, the Back of Beyond. The settlers didn't know much about these territories, except for a few scattered reports that drifted back from Indians or fur trappers who lived west of the Mississippi. Most of the people living in the sixteen states clustered near the Atlantic seaboard put that great wilderness right out of their minds. Thomas Jefferson, on the other hand, looked toward the future and dreamed of westward expansion.

It was a fairly common belief, among well-informed people like the president, that the entire continent could be crossed by water. There was already a navigable route along the Ohio and Mississippi Rivers, stretching from the eastern states to the central part of the continent. And Jefferson had seen a map prepared by a Blackfoot Indian named Ac ko mok ki for the Hudson Bay Company. It showed North America's longest river, the Missouri, flowing from the western banks of the Mississippi all the way to the Rocky Mountains. Then, according to further reports, there was another big river called the Columbia that flowed west from the Rockies into the Pacific Ocean. If this information was true, said Jefferson, the United States could establish trade routes clear across the continent to the Pacific Ocean and the Far East.

In addition to its commercial potential, the western wilderness held great political promise for the president. Jefferson planned to acquire all the territories from the Mississippi River to the Pacific Coast for the United States, thereby extending the country's borders from sea to sea.

The land between the Mississippi and the Rocky Mountains was known as the Louisiana Territory. It had once been claimed by Spain but had recently been surrendered to France as part of an earlier treaty between the two countries. The mountainous region that stretched from the Rockies to the western coast was called the Oregon Country. It was home to North American Indians, but the governments of Spain, France, Russia, and Great Britain were all eager for a share of it.

The first step in President Jefferson's plan for westward expansion was to launch an exploratory expedition. He knew that such an important mission would require a strong leader. The more Jefferson worked with Lewis, the more he grew to like and trust the young man. He decided to ask Meriwether to lead the expedition. In January of 1803, the United States government granted the president $2,500 for his project.

14

A few months later, as luck would have it, Napoléon Bonaparte, the emperor of France, decided to sell the Louisiana Territory to the United States for just under three cents an acre. Napoléon was busy expanding his political power in other parts of the world and had lost interest in North America. In May, Congress ratified a treaty of sale known as the Louisiana Purchase. The United States now owned the very lands that Jefferson's expedition was to cross, at least as far west as the Rockies. As for the Oregon Country, the president intended to negotiate with the Indians after the expedition was completed. Jefferson was confident that they could be persuaded to give up their land, along with their traditional way of life, and live among the white settlers as farmers.

The president had no doubt that Lewis was the right leader for his expedition, and the young man was very proud to be Jefferson's choice. But Lewis knew the job was too big for one person and asked Jefferson's permission to look for a colleague to share the responsibility. The man Lewis had in mind was his old army friend William Clark.

Like Lewis, Clark knew the excitement and adventure of fighting for a new country. He had been born near Richmond, Virginia, on August 1, 1770, the next to last of ten children. When he was still a youngster, his older brother George became a famous general in the American Revolution.

When William was fourteen, his family left Virginia and headed down the Ohio River to establish a homestead in the Kentucky wilderness. Two years later, he joined his brother George in battle against the Shawnee and Wabash Indians, trying to claim their land for white settlers. At twenty-two, William joined the regular army and learned to blaze trails, build bridges, make canoes, and navigate rivers.

On June 19, 1803, Lewis sent a message to Clark. In the very formal language of letters written in those days, he told his friend about the western expedition. It read, "I make this communication to you with the privity of the President who expresses an anxious wish that you would consent to join me in the enterprise." He also asked Clark to start recruiting at nearby army posts for other qualified men to join their party. They needed "some good hunters," Lewis said, "stout, healthy, unmarried men accustomed to the woods and capable of bearing bodily fatigue in a pretty considerable degree."

Eventually, a reply came from Clark. "I do assure you that no man lives with whom I would prefer to undertake such a trip as yourself.... I join you with hand and heart."

Both Meriwether Lewis and William Clark were Virginians by birth. Both were courageous and patriotic. Each one felt the challenge of adventure and discovery, and of defying the unknown. But aside from the few things they had in common, they were about as different as two men could be. William's stocky build and bright red hair matched his friendly, sociable manner. Meriwether's darker coloring and sensitive features reflected a more private personality. Clark liked to be around people. Lewis was a loner.

Although the two men had very different educational backgrounds, their skills and talents complemented each other. Clark had almost no formal schooling, but army training and life in the backwoods of Kentucky had taught him a lot. He was an experienced geographer, mapmaker, nature artist, and river navigator. Lewis had a good basic education, and had been specially tutored in medicine, botany, zoology, and celestial navigation. He also had a strong sense of survival. Lewis and Clark liked and respected each other. Each called the other his friend. Working together, they would prove to be ideal leaders for the expedition.

② A Tall Order

There was much to be done in the coming months, and the preparations that lay ahead must have seemed almost as daunting as the journey itself. Besides wanting the men to find a water route to the Pacific Ocean, President Jefferson instructed Lewis to make friends with the Indians he met along the way and learn about their languages, laws, and customs. Jefferson also told Lewis to make a careful study of the geography, climate, plants, animals, and minerals of each region. He and Clark were to draw accurate maps, by marking latitudes, longitudes, landmarks, and campsites, and they were to keep detailed journals of everything they saw and did. A tall order!

Lewis received final instructions from the president in June of 1803, and in early July he left Washington to buy equipment for the expedition. His first stop was the U.S. Army post at Harpers Ferry, Virginia, where he stocked up on firearms, gunpowder, knives, and tomahawks. His men had to have good weapons for hunting wild game and defending themselves against Indians or fur trappers. From there Lewis went to Philadelphia to buy medical supplies, axes, and a portable blacksmith's forge. All this took time, and he was getting impatient to start the journey west.

The next stop was a shipyard in Pittsburgh, where Lewis had ordered a keelboat. It was to be shaped like a barge, fifty-five feet long and eight feet wide, strong enough to carry up to twelve tons of cargo. It was designed for rowing, towing, poling, or sailing—whatever worked best on the unpredictable rivers.

Finally, at the end of August, the boat was ready. Lewis set off from Pittsburgh, heading south and west on the Ohio River toward the Mississippi. With him was his Newfoundland dog, Scannon. In mid-October, about six hundred miles down the Ohio, Lewis stopped in Kentucky to pick up Clark, along with Clark's black slave York and nine recruits.

At last, in early December, the party arrived in St. Louis, a trading post on the banks of the Mississippi. It was the last white settlement on the edge of the western wilderness and the true starting point of the expedition. Lewis was to stay there long enough to make sure that trunks, tents, bags, boats, and all the rest of their equipment arrived as ordered. Clark took the other men a short distance to Wood River, where they were to remain camped for the rest of the winter.

By early spring, sixteen more volunteers had joined the expedition, and on March 31, 1804, the two captains held a ceremony to enlist all twenty-five recruits. Three men, Floyd, Pryor, and Ordway, held the rank of army sergeant. The other twenty-two were privates. The oldest was thirty-five, the youngest eighteen. The government promised each of the men a few hundred acres of good land when the expedition was completed.

Every man had his own way of doing things, and it was Clark's job to transform them into a closely knit unit. One of the best recruits was George Drouillard, a mixture of French Canadian and Shawnee. He was a good translator, a trusty scout, and could hunt or trap just about anything worth eating. Another valuable member was Pierre Cruzatte, who was part French and part Omaha. He had one eye, knew a lot about navigating a river, and played a mean fiddle.

The other privates included a carpenter, a tailor, a cook, a fisherman, a blacksmith, and a gunsmith.

At last the river ice broke up. "All in health and readiness to set out," Clark wrote in his journal. Boxes, bales, and barrels were loaded into the keelboat and two pirogues, or dugout canoes. Other supplies were strapped onto the backs of four horses. According to Clark's calculations, the stores of flour, sugar, cornmeal, salt pork, whiskey, coffee, animal and plant books, mathematical instruments, medicines, weapons, ammunition, blacksmith tools, camping gear, and personal supplies came to well over 21,000 pounds. The biggest expense in the $2,500 expedition budget was $670 worth of presents for the Indians—handkerchiefs, combs, beads, ribbons, lockets, earrings, needles, pins, thimbles, shirts, blankets, brass kettles, and butcher knives. Only about $350 was spent on basic food supplies. For the most part, the men would live off the land.

It was Monday, May 21, 1804, when the Corps of Discovery, as they now called themselves, rowed across the Mississippi River and headed upstream on the Missouri. Some of the corpsmen walked along the riverbank with the horses, and the rest traveled in the keelboat and the two pirogues. Both dugouts— one painted white, the other painted red—flew the

American flag. Together the two captains and their recruits had all the information and equipment they could possibly have gathered for their journey. But however well prepared they might have been, they had only a hazy idea of what really lay ahead. The expedition was to be full of surprises.

3

Mosquitoes Very Troublesome

It wasn't long before the men of the corps found that everything in the West was bigger and wilder than anything they had known before. The Missouri River, they soon learned, was not just a convenient way to get from one place to another. It was a force to be conquered. According to folklore, the river was made up of four parts water and six parts mud and sand. That's why people called it the Big Muddy. The men had to keep a constant lookout into the cloudy water for snags and sandbars that might tear holes in the boats. Stretches of boulders and rapids were a frequent hazard on the river. One place, where sharp rocks stuck out of the water in every direction, was called the Devil's Race Ground.

On a good day, the expedition logged as many as twenty miles upstream. But often they covered only five or six. When the current was too strong to make any headway at all, the men had to get out of the boats and pull them upstream, using cordelles, or towropes. They walked along the shore, picking their way across slippery mud and jagged rocks. Sudden storms brought driving winds and drenching rains. And nearly every day Clark complained in his journal, "Mosquitoes very troublesome."

In spite of dangers and discomforts, Clark also wrote about the beauty of the land through which they passed. The rugged shoreline smoothed out into grass-covered plains. Springs and brooks bubbled up through the soil. The air was sweet with the smell of shrubs and flowers. "Nature appears to have exerted herself to beautify the scenery," he said.

Each day began with the orderly routine of army life. The corps rose at sunrise, struck camp, and headed upstream, stopping along the way for breakfast and lunch. Food was plentiful. Cornstalks were found scattered in clumps along the riverbanks, and the men ground the kernels for hominy grits or parched them for popping corn. They gathered wild cherries, plums, grapes, and gooseberries by the handful.

York collected whatever wild greens he could find for salads. Nothing was ever wasted, no part of an animal ever thrown away. Hides were sewn into clothing, and bones were cracked for the nutritious marrow inside. Fat was used to make soap and candles or rubbed on skin to keep off mosquitoes and gnats.

During the day, Lewis often walked alone along the riverbank ahead of the others, picking grapes and slapping mosquitoes, listening to the cry of katydids or the thump-thumping of prairie hens. He was happiest when he was alone with his dog, Scannon, who waited patiently while his master stooped down to examine a new plant or scratch in the earth for minerals. Clark, on the other hand, preferred to stay with the boats and make sure his men were doing their jobs.

Every afternoon, toward dusk, scouts walked ahead to look for a good campsite. They had to find a spot that was high enough on the bank so the river's changing currents wouldn't wash them away during the night.

Meanwhile, the hunters went off through the woods or fields on horseback in search of game. Sometimes they shot a deer or elk or bear and hung their quarry from a high tree branch out of reach of wolves. Once the party had found a campsite, the rest of the men secured the boats, pitched the tents, and gathered dry wood for York's cooking fire. If they tired of venison haunch and bear steaks, they ate wild turkey, goose, beaver tail, or buffalo tongue. And when Scannon was in the mood for a swim, he snapped up squirrels in midstream and brought them back for York to toss into the frying pan.

In early August, six hundred miles into their journey, the expedition met a party of Oto and Missouri Indians who lived along the high banks overlooking the river. Following Jefferson's instructions, Lewis held a meeting with the Indians and informed them that the land on which they stood now belonged to the United States and not to Spain or France as in the past. He told them about the white father in Washington who promised they had nothing to fear as long as they cooperated with the government. Clark wrote in his journal that the Indians seemed agreeable to the president's terms. "They were happy that their new father could be depended on." Lewis and Clark called the site of their first meeting Council Bluffs.

Toward the end of September, the corps met the Teton Sioux. It was rumored that these Indians didn't like the white men they had seen so far. But Lewis and Clark had to make friends, or at least make peace, with the tribal leaders before they could cross the Sioux lands and continue west. Negotiations began.

The Sioux chiefs told the corps that they must leave one of the pirogues behind or else turn around and go back home. After much talking and translating back and forth, the Sioux finally let the expedition continue on its way with both pirogues. But good-byes were not very friendly on either side.

As Lewis and Clark made their way up the Missouri, they came across dozens of animals and plants that they had never seen before—badgers, bull snakes, jackrabbits, coyotes, and mule deer. One day they saw a magpie, a bird with blue and green feathers as bright and beautiful as a peacock's. They found a shrub called a buffaloberry, whose fruits York baked into juicy pies. Lewis described each new discovery in his journal, and Clark drew sketches. Following Jefferson's instructions, they carefully collected and preserved plant and animal samples to send back to Washington.

One of their most curious finds was a little creature that looked like a squirrel and barked like a dog. Whole villages of these animals burrowed deep into the ground and built mazes of tunnels nearly a mile long. They poked their heads out of grassy doorways and, if all was safe, darted back and forth visiting each other, whistling and yelping all the while. At the first sign of any danger, they scurried back home and disappeared into their tunnels. The Frenchmen in the corps called the creatures *les petits chiens,* or little dogs, but eventually they came to be known as prairie dogs.

Farther up the river, the trees began to thin out along the banks, and there was little to protect the men from the cold winds that blew across the plains. Except for an occasional view of hills in the distance, the earth was flat, making good grazing land for the buffalo, elk, and goats that were migrating west for the winter.

At long last, in late October of 1804, the expedition came to the Mandan villages that lay along the bluffs of the river near what is now Bismarck, North Dakota. For the next few months, the explorers settled among the four thousand members of the Mandan and Minitaree tribes, the largest cluster of Indians along the Missouri River. Here they planned to spend the winter months until the river ice broke up. The Indians were friendly to all the men of the corps, but they especially liked York. They had never seen a black man before and were sure that he was really a white man with painted skin. They took turns trying to rub off his color. York loved the attention and had fun teasing the Indians. He told them that he was pretty tame now but that he used to be a wild animal.

Then he flashed his teeth, made snorting noises, and rolled his eyes, trying to frighten them. York had a good sense of humor.

The corps kept busy over the winter, restocking game, patching leggings and moccasins, building new dugout canoes, repairing tow ropes, and forging ax blades. The two captains spent long days and nights in their shared hut preparing maps, drawings, reports, and plant and animal specimens for the president.

Although each man had his own style of gathering and recording information, Lewis and Clark worked well together, trying especially hard to separate facts from tall tales. Clark paid close attention to detail and accuracy in his accounts, while Lewis relied more on his own ideas and opinions about the lands through which they traveled. A report written by Clark was usually in the form of lists, charts, and measurements. Lewis often expanded his findings into a thoughtful essay.

The winter months were long and cold. The men of the corps piled on all the warm clothes they could find. Many of the young Indians, on the other hand, were accustomed to the subzero temperatures and ran back and forth on the frozen Missouri, playing a game called lacrosse and wearing almost nothing at all. February brought a few sunny days. At last, in late March, the ice melted from the river. Geese honked over-head, flying north in V-formation.

A few of the men were to return by keelboat to St. Louis with the shipment of boxes, packages, trunks, and cages for President Jefferson. The inventory included a live prairie dog and four live magpies; skeletons of antelope, wolf, and hare; skins of red fox, antelope, bear, and marten; and horns of deer, elk, and mountain ram. Plant and mineral samples were carefully pressed, packed, and labeled with the date and place they had been found. Clark prepared a detailed map of their travels so far and a chart of fifty-three Indian tribes that the expedition had met or heard about. The Mandan contributed tribal buffalo robes, native tobacco, an earthen cooking pot, and an ear of corn.

No value could be placed on such an important ship-ment. If it reached Washington intact, it would tell the eastern settlers more than they had ever imagined about the 1,600 miles the corps had journeyed so far.

4

All the Beasts in the Neighborhood

On the afternoon of April 7, 1805, Lewis and Clark said good-bye to the Mandan. The expedition, now numbering thirty-four, headed up the Missouri in two large pirogues and six smaller canoes. The horses stayed behind. That moment, Lewis wrote, was one of the happiest of his whole life. "This little fleet, although not quite so respectable as those of Columbus or Captain Cook, was still viewed by us with as much pleasure as those deservedly famed adventurers ever beheld theirs." Although the Corps of Discovery was about to cross two thousand miles of unpredictable wilderness, Lewis was confident that the party would be able to complete the president's mission.

Among the new members of the expedition was a

Frenchman named Toussaint Charbonneau, who lived among the Mandan. He had asked to join the corps as a translator. The previous winter Charbonneau had taken as his wife a young Indian woman named Sacajawea, and they now had a two-month-old son. The baby's real name was Jean Baptiste, but everyone called him Pomp. Charbonneau wanted to bring his wife and child along. Most explorers in those days would never have considered including a woman in their party—certainly not a new mother. But Lewis and Clark decided to let her come. Sacajawea had been born into the Shoshone tribe, which lived just east of the Rockies. When she was eleven or twelve years old, she had been captured by a raiding party of Minitaree and taken back to live with them among the Mandan. Sacajawea still spoke her native language and could act as interpreter when the corps reached Shoshone territory, where they hoped to obtain horses and a guide to help them cross the Rockies. The Shoshone woman was a valuable addition to the corps.

When the men set up camp every night along the riverbanks, they began to see tracks of a very large animal. The Mandan had warned them about a huge and powerful beast called a grizzly bear that could maul a man to death in a minute. The grizzly bear, the Indians had said, was not afraid of their arrows.

But the corpsmen reassured themselves that even the most ferocious bear wouldn't stand a chance against rifle bullets. They soon learned, however, that the grizzly had absolutely no fear of humans and that there were places where bears would outnumber men by about ten to one. No wonder scientists called this animal *Ursus horribilis*—horrible bear.

The river was becoming more difficult every day. Its banks rose in jagged cliffs, and huge boulders broke off into the water without warning. Sometimes the shoreline disappeared altogether, and the men had to wade in the slippery riverbed pulling the boats. The towlines, made of elk skin, had started to rot. If they broke, the boats could be smashed to bits on the rocks. When there *was* enough sandy soil along the riverbank to walk on, the men had to make their way through prickly pears, whose sharp thorns pierced even double-thickness moccasins. Sudden gusts of wind blew sand into their eyes, stinging and blinding them. To make matters even worse, many of them suffered from boils and abscesses. "Their labor is incredibly painful and great," Lewis said, "yet these faithful fellows bear it without a murmur."

By June 2, Clark reckoned they had come over 2,500 miles from the expedition's starting point at Wood River. In the 800 miles they had traveled from the Mandan villages, they hadn't seen one other person. At about this time, the expedition came to a big fork in the Missouri. One stream, calm and clear, rolled in from the southwest. The other, churning and muddy, flowed from the northwest. Some reports had said that the north fork was the one to follow, but others believed it was the south. In any case, the corps had heard that there was a big waterfall somewhere on the main river, and once they came to it, they would know they were in the right place. Although Ac ko mok ki's map showed the branching of the Missouri at this point, it didn't give any indication of the falls or the main channel.

It was important that the corps waste no time in deciding which branch to take. The wrong one would lead them way off course, and they would have to retrace their steps. By that time, it would be too late to reach the Rockies before winter, and the heavy snows would make a crossing impossible. Such a mistake, Clark feared, "would probably so dishearten the party that it might defeat the expedition altogether."

On June 4, two scouting parties were formed. Clark's group headed up the south fork, Lewis's up the north fork. Within a few hours Clark was sure he was following the real Missouri. When the two parties met again a few days later, they agreed to explore further. On June 13, Lewis and five of his men set out on foot along the south fork to look for the falls. Later that day, Lewis wrote in his journal, "My ears were saluted with the agreeable sound of a fall of water and, advancing a little further, I saw the spray arise above the plain like a column of smoke." It was a majestic sight, he said, which from the beginning of time had never been seen by a white man. He sent Private Joseph Fields back to Clark with the news and then made camp with the other scouts near the falls. They celebrated that night with a feast of trout, parched cornmeal, and the humps, tongues, and marrowbones of buffalo.

The next morning, Lewis walked alone along the rim of the falls to measure the distance from one end to the other. He soon came to another waterfall, at least fifty feet high. It was one of the most beautiful things he had ever seen. "The water descends in one even and uninterrupted sheet to the bottom where...it rises into foaming billows of great height and rapidly glides away, hissing, flashing, and sparkling." Lewis discovered five falls in all.

It was getting dark, so Lewis headed back to camp, retracing his steps along the falls. He came upon a big herd of grazing buffalo and shot a fat one for his dinner. "While I was gazing attentively on the poor animal," he wrote later, "a large...bear...crept up on me within twenty steps before I discovered him." Lewis drew his rifle. Then he remembered he had used his last bullet on the buffalo. There was no time to reload, no tree or bush to hide behind, and no one to help him. He started to run. The bear lunged after him, full speed ahead. Lewis decided to head for the river. The bear followed. Up to his waist in the water, Lewis looked back and saw the grizzly only twenty feet away. He raised his arm and pointed his spear at the animal, although he didn't have a ghost of a chance of defending himself with it. For some reason, the bear turned tail and ran. Lewis never figured out why, but he was very glad the beast had decided to leave.

A little while later, his rifle reloaded, Lewis came upon a brownish-yellow, catlike creature crouched and ready to spring. He fired his rifle and the animal disappeared. After he had gone a few hundred yards further, Lewis saw another herd of buffalo grazing about half a mile away. Three big bulls separated from the others and charged toward him. A buffalo, like a freight train, takes a little while to work up speed. But once it gets going, the six-foot-tall, two-thousand-pound creature can mow down just about anything in its path.

When the three bulls were close enough to get a good look at Lewis, they changed their minds about trampling him to death and returned to the herd. It seemed, he later complained in his journal, that "all the beasts of the neighborhood had made a league to destroy me." Lewis hurried back to camp as fast as the prickly pear spines that poked at his feet would let him. He didn't stop to dine on the fat buffalo.

Meanwhile, Clark and his party had their own troubles. Several of the men were sick with toothaches and sores, and Sacajawea had developed a high fever. But their good spirits returned when Private Fields arrived with news that Lewis had found the Great Falls of the Missouri, which assured them that the south fork was indeed the main channel of the river.

On June 16, Lewis and his scouts rejoined Clark's party and confirmed the report. However, Lewis told the corps, the sight of these magnificent cascades plunging down the rocky cliffs had destroyed once and for all the hope of finding an all-water route to the Pacific. No boat could survive the falls. The men would have to portage around the falls, carrying their boats and supplies on foot.

⑤

An Impossible Portage

A few days later, the two captains decided that it was time to break camp, head for the falls, and figure out how on earth they were going to make the portage. Clark's job was to chart a course. In order to get around the falls and the rapids between them, the men would have to travel sixteen miles of trail along ground that had been pounded into a hard jagged crust by grazing buffalo. Counting the stretches of rough water on both sides of the falls, the portage would actually cover almost twenty miles. The riverbanks were cut by deep ravines, making matters even more difficult. In fact, Clark wrote in his journal, such a portage was probably impossible. But they had to try, and they were determined to succeed or die in the attempt. "We all believe that we are about to enter on the most perilous and difficult part of our Voyage," Clark said.

Lewis told the men that they must lighten their load by leaving behind the white pirogue and any other equipment they could possibly do without. Cruzatte was in charge of digging a cache, or hiding place, to keep their belongings safe for several years until they returned—if they returned. Then Lewis instructed them to build two wagons to help carry the rest of the gear. There weren't many large trees to choose from, but the men managed to find a cottonwood big enough to saw into wagon wheels. They used the mast of the white pirogue to make axles.

Early in the morning on June 22, the Lewis and Clark expedition began its portage around the Great Falls. The men crossed the rough trail many times, carrying six dugouts and thousands of pounds of equipment. They pushed and tugged load after heavy load, then retraced their steps with the empty wagons to pile on more gear and make the portage yet another time. All the while, they had to endure their "trio of pests," as Lewis called them—gnats, mosquitoes, and prickly pears. Weak from heat and exhaustion, they had to stop and rest often. "At every halt," Lewis wrote, "these poor fellows rumble down and are so much fatigued that many of them are asleep in an instant....Yet no one complains, all go with cheerfulness."

Grizzlies raided their camps every night. The men slept with loaded rifles at their sides and woke often to the warning growls of Scannon on guard duty. Lewis's big dog couldn't keep mice out of the camps, but for some reason the bears respected his territory.

At last, on July 4, 1805, just one year after Lewis had set out from Washington, the Corps of Discovery completed its portage. That night they ate a simple dinner of beans, bacon, buffalo, and suet dumplings. Then, to celebrate Independence Day, their country's twenty-ninth birthday, the two captains passed out the last of the whiskey, and Cruzatte played his fiddle. The men danced and sang and told jokes late into the night. Everyone had a good time but Scannon. The music hurt his ears.

6

Ocean in View!

The corps spent the next week resting and building two more dugouts. By mid-July, the expedition was once again on its way up the Missouri. More than a month had passed since Lewis had first seen the Great Falls, and three months had passed since the men had left the Mandan villages. Only a few weeks remained in which to find Shoshone Indians, bargain for horses and a guide to get them across the Rockies, and begin the trek through the mountains. The crossing had to be completed before winter snows stopped the expedition in its tracks.

The plains were in bloom with yellow and black currants, white-flowering chokecherries, sand rush, wild cucumber, narrow dock, and serviceberries.

Even the pesky prickly pears looked beautiful with their yellow blossoms. Tall, nodding sunflowers were everywhere. Using an old Indian recipe, the men parched the sunflower seeds, pounded them into meal, added enough water or marrow grease to make dough, and baked a very tasty bread.

Before long the expedition left the flat, treeless plains behind. Rising from the banks of the Missouri, the eastern slopes of the Rockies were covered with clumps of pine, cedar, and balsam. In one place, near what is now the city of Helena, Montana, sheer cliffs of black granite and cream-colored flint rose 1,200 feet on either side of the river. Lewis called them the "gates of the Rocky Mountains." Mosquitoes and gnats were as bothersome as ever, and scattered among the ever-present prickly pear thorns were sharp slivers of flint that tore the men's moccasins and cut their feet. Clark was sick with aches and fever, and all the men were hot, tired, bitten, and bruised as they continued on in search of Shoshone.

Toward the end of July, the explorers came to three big forks in the river. Lewis and Clark named them the Jefferson, the Madison, and the Gallatin, after the president and his secretaries of state and treasury. It was here that Sacajawea recognized the exact spot where her tribe had been camped when she was taken prisoner five years earlier. They followed the Jefferson, which was obviously the main stream.

By early August, the explorers were already several hundred miles into the eastern range of the Rockies. Lewis grew more and more discouraged as each day passed without any sign of Shoshone. "If we do not find them," he said, "I fear the successful issue of our voyage will be very doubtful." On August 11, Lewis and a small scouting party spotted an Indian in the distance. As they approached to offer a friendly greeting, the Indian turned his horse and rode away, apparently suspicious or afraid of the strangers.

Frustrated and disappointed, Lewis and his men continued along the narrowing path of the river. Soon they came to a sight that few, if any, white men had ever seen before—the trickling source of the Missouri. They sat on the bank to rest and drink the clear, icy water. Lewis wrote in his journal that they had at last reached "the most distant fountain of the waters of the mighty Missouri in search of which we have spent so many toilsome days and restless nights."

On August 12, Lewis's party followed an old Indian road, hoping to find the source of the Columbia River. They walked along the trail to the top of a ridge for a better view of whatever lay to the west. When they reached the crest of the ridge, Lewis realized that they were standing on the Great Continental Divide, where the rivers behind them flowed east to the Atlantic and the ones before them ran west to the Pacific.

The following day, Lewis and his party were scouting on foot when they met two Shoshone women. At first the women were frightened, but Lewis assured them, through signs and gestures, that his men were friendly. The women agreed to lead the party to the Shoshone camp. When they had walked together for two miles, they came upon a group of sixty warriors on horseback. Lewis set his rifle on the ground to show them that his mission was peaceful. When the warriors saw that the scouts had brought presents, their chief approached Lewis on foot, saying, *"ah-hi-e, ah-hi-e,"* which means, "I am much pleased." The chief greeted Lewis in the customary fashion, throwing an arm around the captain's shoulder and touching Lewis's cheek with his own.

The Indians embraced each of the men, smearing their cheeks with grease paint from their own faces. Then they continued on to their camp, where Lewis and the Shoshone chief, Cameahwait, smoked a traditional peace pipe. Over the next few days, the Indians and Lewis's scouts grew to trust each other. Although their food supply was low and they had few possessions, the Shoshone were cheerful and generous.

They were especially curious about the peculiar skin color of the new strangers, whose tanned faces were the same deep brown as theirs, but whose arms, under their shirt sleeves, were white.

A short time later, a group of Shoshone, including Chief Cameahwait, accompanied Lewis back to the spot where he was to meet Clark. It wasn't long before Clark, Sacajawea, and the rest of the party, carrying the canoes and most of the gear, arrived at the appointed meeting place. As Sacajawea came closer to the Shoshone, she began to dance and suck on her fingers. "These are my people," she was saying in sign language. "They nursed me as a child."

Lewis called a meeting to ask Cameahwait for horses and a guide to help the expedition cross the westernmost, and highest, range of the Rockies. In return, the Shoshone would be given a supply of firearms at some time in the future. Sacajawea was asked to interpret. The chief began to talk and everyone waited for the young woman to translate. Sacajawea was silent. She sat very still and stared into the long lean face and piercing eyes of the chief. Then to everyone's amazement, she jumped up, hugged Cameahwait, and threw her blanket over him. Sacajawea was giving a traditional Shoshone greeting, for she had recognized the chief as her brother.

A few days later, August 18, was Lewis's thirty-first birthday. In spite of the great success of the expedition so far, he was feeling depressed, as he sometimes did. He wrote in his journal that he had "done but little . . . to further the happiness of the human race or to advance the information of the succeeding generation."

It was the end of August when the Corps of Discovery left the Shoshone camp with twenty-nine horses, a mule, and Cameahwait's guide, Old Toby. The Missouri River had trickled out to nothing, and as yet, there was no other navigable river that flowed into the Columbia. Old Toby was to lead them along the old Indian trails through the mountains.

The days ahead were the worst of the whole expedition. High winds brought trees crashing down across the trails. Snow and frost covered the ground. Horses slipped and rolled down the steep, icy slopes. There was no game, and although Sacajawea found wild fruits and vegetables, these weren't nearly enough to give the men the strength they needed. Soon they were sick and exhausted and as skinny as scarecrows. Lewis began to doubt that luck was still with them. Clark complained of being wetter and colder than he had ever been in his life.

Late in September, the expedition finally came to Lolo

Pass, the gateway to their final descent down the western slopes of the mountains. The corps made a mental note to tell President Jefferson that the trek across the Rockies was quite a bit more than the brisk hike he had predicted. Even Old Toby lost his way twice and eventually deserted the expedition altogether.

Before long the corps came to an Indian village that no white person had ever seen before. Some of the tribe's members wore shells in their pierced noses. The white men called the tribe Nez Perce, which comes from the French phrase *nez percé,* or pierced nose. The Nez Perce were friendly and welcoming, and helped the explorers restock their supplies. Early in October, the expedition set off again with restored energy, accompanied by two Nez Perce guides, Chief Twisted Hair and Chief Tetoharsky. They also brought with them forty of the village dogs, a staple of the Indians' diet. Clark never did get used to eating dog meat, but Lewis liked it even better than elk or venison and said it made his men strong and healthy.

Equipped with new dugouts, Lewis and Clark planned to continue their journey on the Snake River, which raced from the western foothills of the Rockies to join the Columbia. But when they saw the narrow stream twisting its way through boulders and canyons, they became discouraged. Another portage.

Cruzatte, however, wanted to try his luck on the river. The rest of the men watched from the steep banks as he steered each of the loaded canoes through the angry rapids, without so much as a scratch to either man or boat. There was a big party in camp that night. Cruzatte fiddled and Scannon whimpered.

Over the next few days, the men could tell that they were entering new territory, the waters of the Columbia. Rocks and rapids disappeared and the river grew calm as it widened. In place of canyon walls were forests of giant spruce trees. The biggest ones were two hundred feet tall and ten to fifteen feet thick. Pacific salmon swam in the river, and the water level rose and fell as the ocean's tides pushed inland and then pulled back to sea. Even the Indians along the way were different. They were used to white men and had often traded with them. The Indians wore British navy jackets and tried out their English words on the white people who went by.

When the Corps of Discovery rose on the morning of November 7, 1805, the fog was so thick they couldn't see the other side of the river. The men broke camp and started downstream. Out of the silent morning came a faraway roar like thunder. It was the sound of waves pounding on a rocky coastline. It was the sound that told them they had made it to the Pacific at last.

The men rowed on, past a string of Indian villages along the banks. Just as they came to the last village, the fog lifted and the Lewis and Clark expedition saw the ocean in the distance. "That ocean," Clark said, was "the object of all our labors, the reward of all our anxieties." The men began to sing and shout, and Clark reached for his journal to make the most important entry of all. "Ocean in view! O! The joy!"

Afterword

The telephone and telegraph hadn't been invented yet, and the western territories wouldn't have any postal service for many years to come. So there was no way for Lewis and Clark to send word back to the president. "The Pacific at last!" "Mission accomplished!" "We've done it!" These might have been their messages of triumph, pride, and relief. But they would have to wait. Meanwhile, the president had heard no news of the expedition for quite some time and feared that all the men were dead. The corps, however, had lost only one member. Sergeant Floyd had died of a burst appendix in August of 1804.

Lewis and Clark could only guess how disappointed Jefferson would be to hear that there was no all-water route from the Atlantic to the Pacific. But they would assure the president that with a combination of waterways and overland trails, the continent could indeed be crossed all the way from sea to sea. And they would be able to present him with accurate maps, charts, and journals, along with detailed descriptions and beautiful drawings of 122 animals, 178 plants, and 24 Indian tribes that white settlers had never heard of before.

Battling boredom, rain, and fleas, the Corps of Discovery spent the winter of 1805–06 on the Pacific Coast, near what is now Astoria, Oregon. They camped among the Clatsop and Chinook Indians. Then came spring and the journey back home. On September 23, 1806, almost two and a half years after they left their camp at Wood River in May of 1804, the men of the corps, dressed in buckskins, straggled back into St. Louis. They had journeyed eight thousand miles in all, a third of the Earth's circumference. A festive welcome lasted for many days.

At last Lewis was able to send word to President Jefferson, whose reply began, "I received, my dear Sir, with unspeakable joy your letter of September 23..." The corps learned that the shipment sent from the Mandan villages in the spring of 1805 had safely reached the president a few months later. Jefferson especially liked the Indian artifacts and kept them at Monticello. Many of the animal and mineral samples were placed in a museum in Philadelphia, and the plants were sent to botanists all around the country for further study.

Not long after the president sent his reply to Lewis, he summoned Meriwether Lewis and William Clark to Washington, where the nation cheered and honored them as heroes.

In the years following the expedition, Lewis was appointed governor of the Upper Louisiana Territory. He died mysteriously in October of 1809. Some people thought he was murdered, but it's more likely that he was suffering from depression and took his own life. Clark served for many years as Superintendent of Indian Affairs and was especially concerned with protecting Indian tribal land rights. Pomp, the youngest member of the expedition, was educated in Europe at Clark's expense and became a well-known western guide and interpreter. One of the western travelers who hired him in later years was Clark's own son Jefferson.

The Lewis and Clark journals were edited, published, and republished many times, and are still read today for their spirit of adventure, courage, and leadership.

Bibliography

Ambrose, Stephen E. *Undaunted Courage: Meriwether Lewis, Thomas Jefferson, and the Opening of the American West.* New York: Simon & Schuster, 1996.

Bakeless, John. *The Adventures of Lewis and Clark.* Boston: Houghton Mifflin, 1962.

Bergon, Frank, ed. *The Journals of Lewis and Clark.* New York: Penguin, 1989.

Chidsey, Donald Barr. *Lewis and Clark: The Great Adventure.* New York: Crown, 1970.

Fitz-Gerald, Christine A. *Meriwether Lewis and William Clark.* Chicago: Children's Press, 1991.

Hawke, David Freeman. *Those Tremendous Mountains: The Story of the Lewis and Clark Expedition.* New York: W.W. Norton, 1980.

Howard, Harold P. *Sacajawea.* Norman, Okla.: University of Oklahoma Press, 1971.

Moodie, D.W. and Barry Kaye. "The Ac Ko Mok Ki Map." *The Beaver* 307, no. 4 (1977): 5-15.

Snyder, Gerald S. *In the Footsteps of Lewis and Clark.* Washington, D.C.: National Geographic Society, 1970.

Viola, Herman J. *Exploring the West.* Washington, D.C.: Smithsonian Books, 1987.

Index